4

DILLARD SCHOOL

BLUE

HBJ SCIENCE

AUTHORS

ELIZABETH K. COOPER
formerly Coordinator of Teacher Training
University of California

PAUL E. BLACKWOOD
formerly Specialist for Science Education
U.S. Office of Education*

JOHN A. BOESCHEN
formerly Science Teacher, Pinole, California

MORSLEY G. GIDDINGS
Professor of Education
Brooklyn College, City University of New York

ARTHUR A. CARIN
Professor of Elementary and Early Childhood Education
and Director of Environmental Education
Queens College, City University of New York

*The work of Paul E. Blackwood was done in his
private capacity, and no official endorsement by the
U.S. Office of Education is intended or should be inferred.

CONSULTING SPECIALISTS
IN THE SCIENCES

GARRETT HARDIN, *Biology and Ecology*
Emeritus Professor of Human Ecology
University of California, Santa Barbara

RICHARD C. LEWONTIN, *Biology and Genetics*
Professor, Harvard University, Cambridge, Massachusetts

ALISTAIR W. McCRONE, *Geology and Earth Science*
Professor of Geology
Humboldt State University, Arcata, California

FRANKLIN MILLER, JR., *Physics*
Emeritus Professor of Physics
Kenyon College, Gambier, Ohio

SYDNEY B. NEWELL, *Chemistry*
President, CompEditor, Inc., Chapel Hill, North Carolina

FLETCHER G. WATSON,
Astronomy and Science Education
Emeritus Professor, Harvard University,
Cambridge, Massachusetts

HARCOURT BRACE JOVANOVICH, PUBLISHERS
Orlando   New York   San Francisco
Chicago   Atlanta   Dallas

CONTENTS: Units 1, Jim Cartier, Photo Researchers; 2, E.R. Degginger, Earth Scenes; 3, William H. Calvert, E.R. Degginger; 4, HBJ Photo; 5, Peter Southwick, Stock Boston; 6, Jack Parson, OPC; 7, Steve Wilson, Entheos; 8, J. Alex Langley, DPI; 9, Triangli, Palmer, DPI; 10, Jon Yeager, Photo Library; 11, Phil Rymer.

ILLUSTRATORS: Philip M. Veloric, Publisher's Graphics, Artists International, Mulvey Associates.

PICTURE ACKNOWLEDGMENTS

Key: (t) top, (b) bottom, (l) left, (r) right, (c) center.

HBJ PHOTOS: Pages 3 (bl), 4 (bl) (br), 5, 6 (cl) (tr) (br), 8, 9, 14 (tl) (bl), 15, 18 (insets), 19 (insets), 20, 21 (tl) (cr), 22, 26, 41, 44 (t), 53, 60, 61, 69 (tr), 70 (tl) (tr) (bc), 72 (b), 79, 80 (tr) (b), 81, 82, 83 (tr) (bl), 84, 86 (tl) (tr) (bl), 91, 93, 97, 103, 106, 107, 110 (b), 114, 115 (tl) (bl) (tr), 117, 118, 119, 120, 121, 124 (tr) (bl) (br), 129, 131, 132, 133, 134, 136 (c), 146.

RESEARCH PHOTOS: Pages vi: (tl) Jim Cartier, Photo Researchers; (tr) Eric Hausserman, Photo Researchers; (b) Susan McCartney, Photo Researchers. 1: (l) Lea, Omni Photo Communications; (tr) B. Mitchell, The Image Bank; (br) Robert Knowles, Photo Researchers. 2: (tl) Cary Wolinsky, Stock Boston; (tr) Ann Hagen Griffith, Omni Photo Communications; (bl) Erika Stone, Peter Arnold; (br) Pam Hasegawa, Taurus Photos. 3: (tl) Whitney L. Lane, The Image Bank; (tr) Richard Hutchings, Photo Researchers; (br) B. Kreye, The Image Bank. 4: (tl) Focus On Sports; (tr) Bruce Roberts, Photo Researchers; (cr) Richard Hutchings, Photo Researchers. 6: (tl) Peter Southwick, Stock Boston; (bl) Kenneth Karp. 7: (tr) Pam Hasegawa, Taurus Photos; (br) Elaine Wicks, O.S.R., Taurus Photos. 14: (r) Dr. E. R. Degginger, Earth Scenes. 16: (tl) Dr. E. R. Degginger; (bl) Grant Heilman; (tr) Grant Heilman; (cr) Manuel Rodriguez; (br) Alan Pitcairn, Grant Heilman; (br) L. L. T. Rhodes, Earth Scenes. 17: (tl) Bruce A. MacDonald, Earth Scenes; (cl) William E. Ferguson; (tr) (bl) Grant Heilman; (br) Cary Wolinsky, Stock Boston. 19: (tl) (b) Grant Heilman; (tr) Cary Wolinsky, Stock Boston. 21: (tr) Robert Shepperd, Photo Library; (b) Jim Brandenburg, Photo Library. 24: (tl) Freida Leinwand/Monkmeyer; (bl) (br) Grant Heilman; (tr) Dr. E. R. Degginger. 25: Sybil Shelton, Peter Arnold. 28-29: William Calvert, Dr. E. R. Degginger. 30: (t) Fritz Prenzel, Bruce Coleman; (bl) George and Judy Manna, Photo Researchers; (c) Hal H. Harrison, Grant Heilman; (br) Grant Heilman. 31: (tl) Dr. E. R. Degginger; (bl) Tom McHugh, Photo Researchers; (tr) Richard Kolar, Animals Animals; (cr) Breck P. Kent, Animals Animals; (br) Stephen Dalton, Animals Animals. 32: (tl) George H. Harrison, Grant Heilman; (cl) Gunter Ziesler, Peter Arnold; (bl) Leonard Lee Rue III, The Image Bank; (br) Charles Palek, Tom Stack & Associates; (br) W. Perry Conway, Grant Heilman. 34: (t) Jen and Des Bartlett, Bruce Coleman; (b) Grant Heilman. 35: Zig Leszcynski, Animals Animals. 36: (tl) Leonard Lee Rue III, Tom Stack & Associates; (tr) Malcolm S. Kirk, Peter Arnold; (rc) Oxford Scientific Films, Animals Animals; (b) Hans Rheinhard, Bruce Coleman. 37: (t) Lynn M. Stone, Animals Animals; (bl) Marc N. Boulton, Bruce Coleman; (br) Grant Heilman. 38: (tl) Isidor Jeklin, Animals Animals; (tr) Esao Hashimoto, Animals Animals; (b) Norman Myers, Bruce Coleman. 39: (tl) Warren Garst, Tom Stack & Associates; (tr) Dr. E. R. Degginger; (b) Wildlife Photographers, Bruce Coleman. 40: (tl) Raymond A. Mendez, Animals Animals; (b) Dr. E. R. Degginger. 42: (tl) Animals Animals; (bl) Thomas Houland, Grant Heilman; (tr) David C. Fritts, Animals Animals; (br) Grant Heilman. 44: (bl) Margaret W. Peterson, The Image Bank; (br) C. Allan Morgan, Peter Arnold. 45: (l) John Running, Photo Library; (tr) B. Kreye, The Image Bank; (tr) Bob Firth, Photo Library. 46: Dr. E. R. Degginger. 47: (tl) Harry Engels, Animals Animals; (tr) Michael Nabicht, Animals Animals; (b) R. F. Head, Animals Animals. 48: (tl) F. E. Unverhau, Animals Animals; (bl) Marty Stouffer, Animals Animals; (r) Leonard Lee Rue III, Animals Animals. 49: (t) Leonard Lee Rue III, Animals Animals; (bl) Gary W. Griffin, Animals Animals; (br) Ronald Orenstein, Animals Animals. 50: (tl) Hans Reinhard, Bruce Coleman; (tr) Marion Austerman, Animals Animals; (b) Helen Williams, Photo Researchers. 51: (t) Hans Reinhard, Bruce Coleman; (b) Russ Kinne, Photo Researchers. 52: (t) Andy Young, Photo Researchers; (bl) Alan G. Nelson, Animals Animals; (br) Zig Leszcynski, Animals Animals. 54: (t) Werner Meinel, Taurus Photos; (c) Scott Ransom, Taurus Photos; (b) Carl Purcell, Photo Researchers. 56: (tl) Christina Dittmann, Rainbow; (bl) Grant Heilman. 56-57: (c) Guido Alberto Rossi, The Image Bank. 57: (tr) Peter Southwick, Stock Boston; (br) Christina Dittmann, Rainbow. 58: (t) John Serras, Photo Researchers; (b) Bill Noel Kleeman, Tom Stack & Associates. 59: Dr. E. R. Degginger. 62: Grant Heilman. 63: Bill Gause, Photo Researchers. 64: Dennis Fisher, International Stock Photo. 65: Grant Heilman. 66: (b) Manuel Rodriguez; (bc) Thomas Ives. 66-67: (t) Grant Heilman. 67: (bl) Zig Leszcynski, Animals Animals; (tr) Dr. E. R. Degginger; (br) Stephen J. Krasemann, Photo Researchers. 68: (tl) Michal Heron; (bl) Manuel Rodriguez; (br) Dr. E. R. Degginger, Earth Scenes. 69: (tl) W. K. Almond, Stock Boston; (tr) Dr. E. R. Degginger. 70: (bl) Sybil Shackman, Monkmeyer. 72: (t) Manuel Rodriguez; (c) Grant Heilman. 74: (t) L. L. T. Rhodes, Taurus Photos; (bl) Wil Blanche, DPI; (br) Phoebe Dunn, DPI. 75: (l) Ann Hagen Griffiths, Omni Photo Communications; (tr) Jack Parsons, Omni Photo Communications; (br) Michal Heron, Woodfin Camp & Associates. 78: (l) Ray Solowinski, International Stock Photo; (r) Manley Photo, Shostal Associates. 80: (tl) Charles E. Schmidt, Taurus Photos. 83: (tl) Glyn Cloyd, Taurus Photos; (br) Robert Rattner. 85: Bob Evans, Peter Arnold. 86: (br) Annie Griffiths, Photo Library. 88: (tl) Myron Wood, Photo Researchers; (bl) Stephen J. Krasemann, Photo Library. 88-89: (c) Tom Tracy, Alpha Photo. 89: (tr) Steve Wilson, Entheos. 92: Edward Lettau, Peter Arnold. 94: Tom Stack. 95: (l) Farrell Grehan, Photo Researchers; (tr) Daniel Brody, Stock Boston; (br) Dana Hyde, Photo Researchers. 98: Stephen J. Krasemann, Peter Arnold; (b) Jerome Wyckoff, Earth Scenes. 100-101: J. Alex Langley, DPI. 102: William E. Ferguson. 108: Peter Southwick, Stock Boston. 109: (l) Joshua Tree, Editorial Photocolor Archives; (r) Frederic Lewis, Inc. 110: (t) George H. Harrison, Grant Heilman. 112: (tl) Carter L. Hamilton, DPI; (bl) Phoebe Dunn, DPI; (tr) Triangli/Palmeri, DPI. 112-113: (b) Ann Hagen Griffiths, Omni Photo Communications. 113: (t) Alec Duncan, Taurus Photos; (br) Jack Parsons, Omni Photo Communications. 115: (br) Pam Hasegawa, Taurus Photos. 122: (tl) Frederik D. Bodin, Stock Boston; (bl) Lenore Weber, Omni Photo Communications; (cr) Dr. E. R. Degginger, Earth Scenes; (br) Robert A. Isaacs, Photo Researchers. 123: Bill Grimes, Leo de Wys. 124: (tl) Michal Heron, Monkmeyer. 126: Jerry Downs, Photo Library. 127: (l) Nick Nicholson, The Image Bank; (r) Jon Yeager, Photo Library. 128: (tl) Mimi Forsyth, Monkmeyer; (r) Frank Siteman, Stock Boston. 135: Dr. E. R. Degginger, Earth Scenes. 136: (t) Larry Trone, DPI; (b) Hugh Rogers, Monkmeyer. 145: (tl) C. Allan Morgan, Peter Arnold; (tr) Courtesy, Field Museum of Natural History, Chicago; (b) Tom McHugh, Photo Researchers. 147: The American Museum of Natural History. 150: Courtesy, The Los Angeles County Museum. 151: Michael Collier, Stock Boston. 152: Courtesy, Field Museum of Natural History, Chicago.

PRINTED IN THE UNITED STATES OF AMERICA

ISBN 0-15-365490-2

Contents

iv

BLUE

HBJ SCIENCE

Growing Up
Healthy

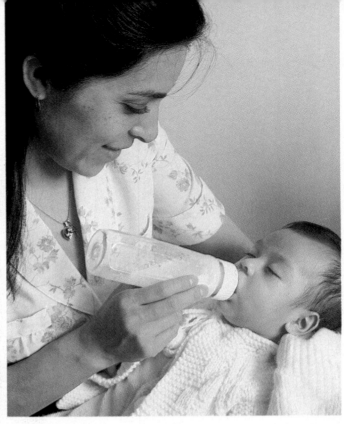
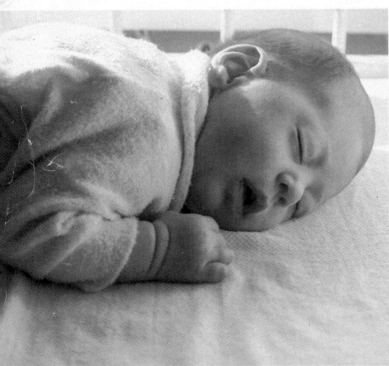
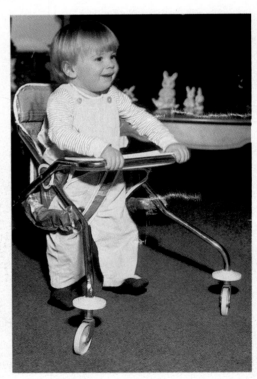

You were small.

2

Now you are bigger.
What can you do now?

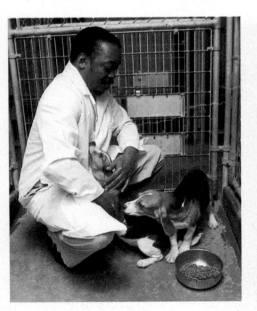

You will grow up.

What can you do then?

Find Out How Tall You Are.

Do this with a friend.

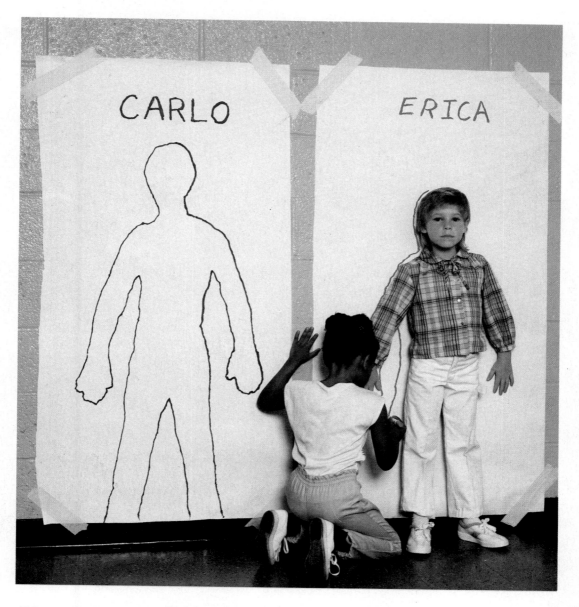

Is everyone the same?

What keeps you healthy?

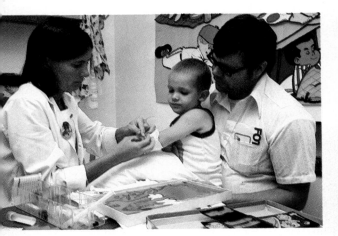

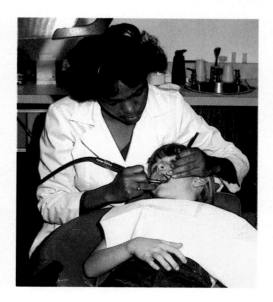

Food helps you to grow.

What foods are good for you?

Where Does Our Food Come From?

Find or draw pictures of foods.
Find or draw pictures that show
where foods come from.

You grow.

Your feet grow, too.

Who helps you get shoes that fit?

You grow and change.

You need to sleep.

You need to play.

You need to eat
good foods.

Which things do you use
when you are bigger?

Which keep you healthy?

13

More and More Plants

There are many kinds of plants.

How are they different?

17

Many plants grow
from seeds.
A seed grows its own
kind of plant.

18

What kind of plant will
grow from each seed?

19

What Do Seeds Need to Grow?

Plant 3 seeds in each cup.

Put water in cup A each day.

Do not put water in cup B.

What happens?

How do plants get water?

What Do Plants Need to Grow?

Put a plant in the light.
Put a plant in the dark.
Water them each day.
What will happen?

This plant gets light.
It gets water.
Is it growing?

This plant gets no light.
It gets water.
Is it growing?
Why?

Plants grow in many places.

Where do you see plants grow?

This man works with plants.

He knows what plants need.

Many plants grow
from seeds.

There are many kinds of
seeds.

Each seed grows its own
kind of plant.

Plants need soil and
water.

Plants need light.

What will grow from each seed?

What do plants need to grow?

More and More Animals

There are many kinds of animals.
How are these animals different?

Tell how these animals
move around.

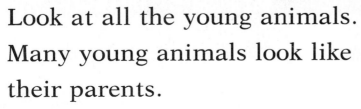

Look at all the young animals.
Many young animals look like
their parents.

32

Make a Home for This Animal.

Keep it in a warm place.

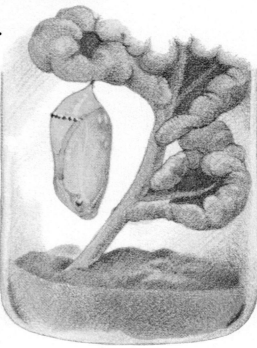

What happens?

Some animals hatch from eggs.
What animals are hatching?

These animals are mammals.

Mammals do not hatch from eggs.

They are born ready to move.

Which of these mammals
do you know?

Some animals take care
of their young.

These young animals get
their own food.

They take care of themselves.

Have you ever seen these animals?

This woman owns the pet store.

What animals would you find there?

41

Many young animals look like their parents.

Some animals hatch from eggs.

Mammals do not hatch from eggs.

Some animals take care of their young.

Which look like their parents?

Which hatch from eggs?

Which take care of their young?

Living and Growing

44

What are the animals doing?

Why?

Animals need food and water.
Animals need a place to live.

Where do these animals live?

Young animals grow as
big as their parents.

Which animal will grow biggest?

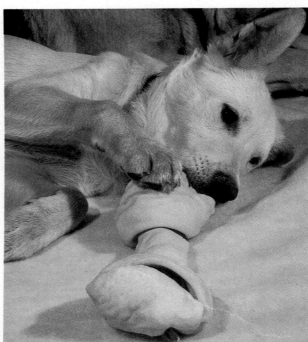

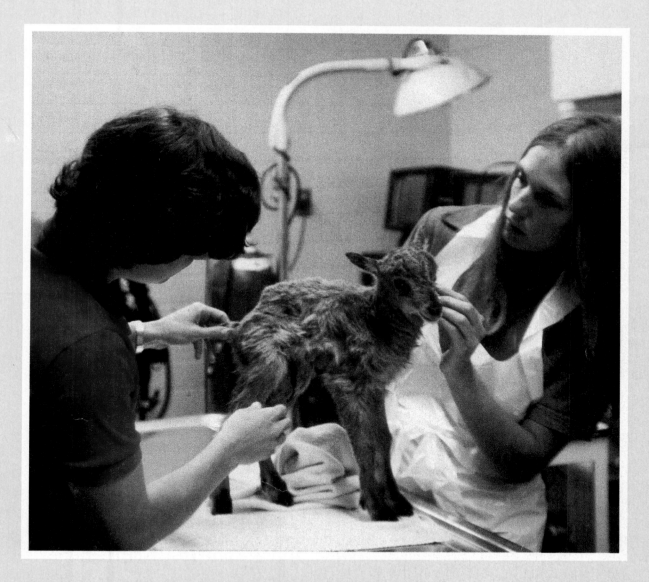

Who helps this animal
stay healthy?

Animals need food
and water.

Animals need a
place to live.

Young animals grow as
big as their parents.

54

Which show what animals need?

Which animal will grow biggest?

Earth, Our Home

57

The insects eat small plants.

Fish eat the insects.

This animal eats fish.

Animals need food.

Where do they get their food?

Do animals and plants need each other?

Make a Home for Fish.

Put in sand.
Put in water.
Put in small
rocks.

Put in plants.
Put in snails
and fish.

Feed the fish each day.

Do animals and plants need each other?

Insects lived here.
So people sprayed around the lake.
The insects died.

Some spray got into the lake.
It made some fish sick.

The owl comes to the lake.

It eats fish.

What might happen to the owl?

We need clean air to live.
We need clean water, too.

The air and land are dirty here.

The water is dirty, too.

What might happen to people?

There are very few of these plants.
There are very few of these animals.

People try to save them.

Earth is home for all living things.

We must take care of the Earth.

How can we help take care of our Earth?

How does he help take
care of our Earth?

Plants and animals
need each other.

We need clean
air and water.

Dirty water and air
can make living
things sick.

We must take care
of our Earth.

Tell how these animals
get their food.

Find the things that
can make us sick.

What can we do to help?

Matter All Around You

75

All things are made of matter.
The glass and wood are matter.

What else is made of matter?

There are three forms of matter.
Solids are one form of matter.
These are solids.

Solids can be small.
Solids can be large.

Solids can be hard.
Solids can be soft.
All solids have a shape.

What shapes do you
see here?

Liquids are another form of matter.

You can pour a liquid.
Do liquids change shape?

Gases are matter, too.

Air is a gas.

You cannot see air.

Wave your hands fast.

Do you feel air moving?

What is air doing
in each picture?

Is the Glass Empty?

Put a glass in water like this.

Tip the glass slowly.
What comes out of the glass?
What are the bubbles made of?

What matter does a diver use?

All things are made of matter.

There are three
forms of matter.

Solids are one form
of matter.

Liquids are another
form of matter.

Gases are matter, too.

Which are made of matter?

Which are solids?

Which are liquids?

Where are the gases?

Rain and Shine

Some days it rains.

Some days it does not rain.

Does It Rain Where You Live?

Make a chart.
Show the kind of day it is.

Rain comes from clouds.

Look at the little cloud.
It is made of tiny
drops of water.

Have you ever seen
clouds like these?

Big clouds are made
of tiny drops of water, too.

Water goes into the air.
Where do clouds get water?

The Sun helps water
go into the air.

Which Will Dry Faster?

Put a little water on each plate.

Which will dry faster?

96

Who tells you if it will rain?

Some clouds
bring rain.

Clouds are made of
tiny drops of water.

Clouds get water
from many places.

The Sun helps water
go into the air.

Where does rain come from?

What are clouds made of?

Where do clouds get water?

What makes water go into the air?

Day and Night

101

We get light and heat
from the Sun.

We have day.
Is it always day?

We have night.
Is it always night?

The Sun is lighting part
of the Earth.

Part of the Earth is dark.
That part has night.

Find Out About Day and Night.

Where is it day?

Where is it night?

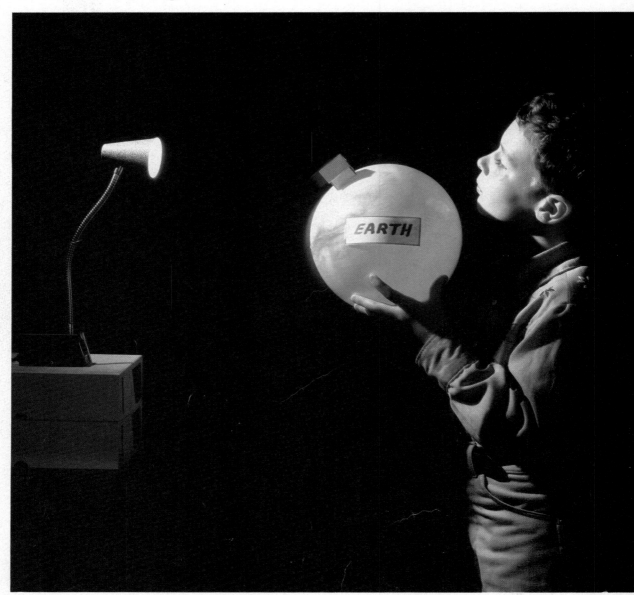

Turn the Earth this way.

Now where is it day?

Where is it night?

Why do we have day and night?

The Earth turns all the time.
Soon it will be dark here.
Why?

Some people work in the day.
Some people work at night.
They keep you safe day and night.

We get light and heat
from the Sun.

We have day and night
because the Earth turns.

110

Which gives off light and heat?

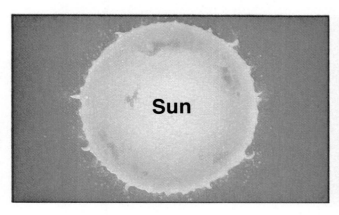

What happens when the Sun
shines on the Earth?

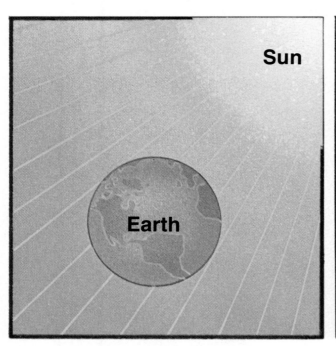

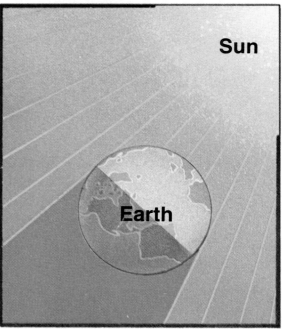

Push and Pull

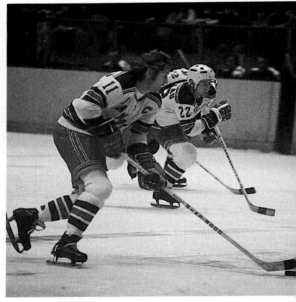

113

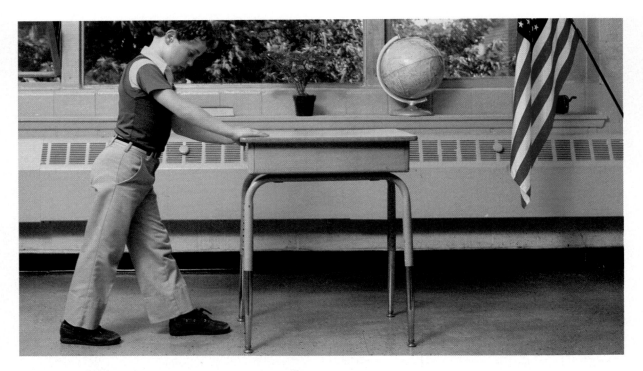

A push can move something.

A pull can move something.

Which people are pushing?
Which people are pulling?

Which takes more force?

Why?

Which Takes More Force?

Push the book.

Push the books.

Which takes more force?
Why?

Where is it easier to move?

Which Is Easier to Move?

Pull it.

Pull it now.

Which is easier to move?
Why?

119

Which way is easier?

Wheels Help Us.

Push the truck.

Push it now.

Which is easier?
Why?

We use wheels at
work and play.

These people make buildings.

Do they use wheels?

Do they push and pull?

A push or pull can move something.

Heavy things take
more force to move.

It is easy to move
things here.

It is not easy to
move things here.

Wheels make things
easier to move.

124

Which takes more force?

Where is it easier to move?

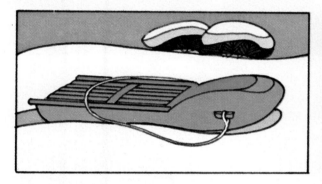
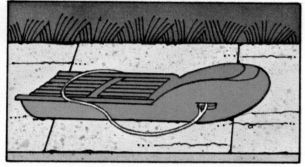

Which way is easier?

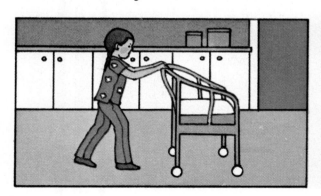
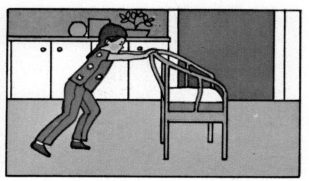

Down and Up

What makes them come down?

Gravity pulls them down.
It takes force to lift them.

Which takes more force to lift?
Why?

Which is easier?

Inez goes up the stairs.

Bert goes down the stairs.

Which is easier?

Magnets can lift things.

How do we use magnets?

What Can a Magnet Lift?

Touch things with a magnet.

What can a magnet lift?

Make a chart to show these things.

The crane has a big magnet.
What does the magnet lift?

Gravity pulls
things down.

It takes force to
lift things.

Heavy things take
more force to lift.

Magnets can lift
some things.

What makes them come down?

Which takes more force to lift?

Which can a magnet lift?

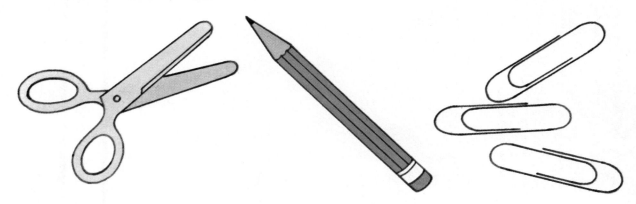

Earth, Long Ago

139

The Earth was different
long ago.

The plants were different, too.

Dinosaurs lived on the Earth
long, long ago.

Have you ever seen a dinosaur?

The mammoth lived long ago.
It was big and hairy.
Does it look like an
animal you know?

Cave people hunted them
for food and clothing.

The mammoths died out long ago.

The saber-toothed cat
lived long ago.

Does it look like an
animal you know?

How do we know about animals
that lived long ago?

Make a Model Fossil.

Press something in the clay.
Let the clay dry.
Cover the fossil with sand.

Let a friend find the fossil.
Let a friend guess what it is.

How do we know about mammoths?

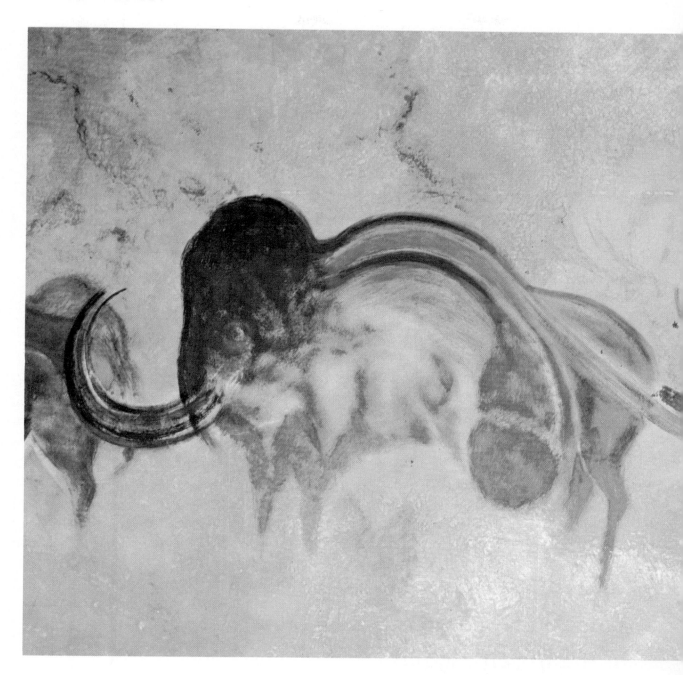

This young mammoth was found
in the frozen ground.

How did it keep so long?

Animals came to tar pools
many years ago.

Some got stuck.
What do you think happened?

People found bones in the tar.
The bones came from an animal.

Can you tell what kind
of animal it was?

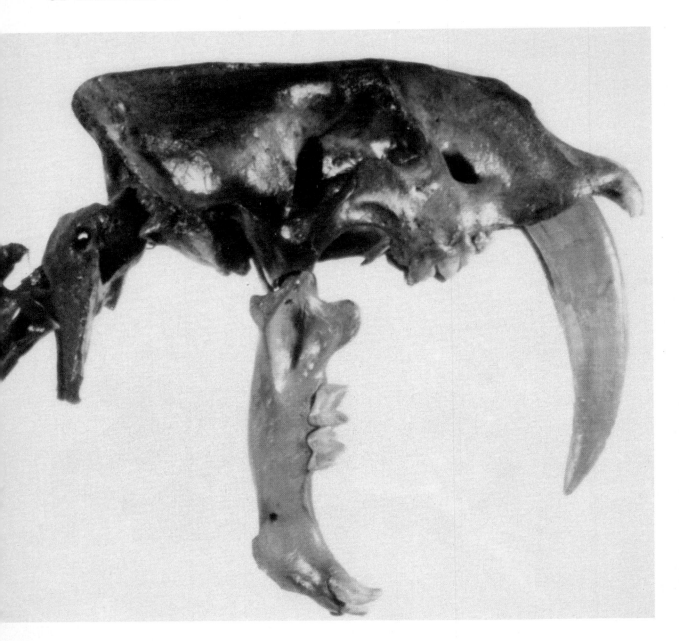

How do scientists find out
about animals of long ago?

The Earth was different long ago.

Many animals died out.

We know about these animals from fossils.

What was the Earth like long ago?

Which animals died out?

How do we know about animals
that lived long ago?

153

Science Words

air, 64

animals, 30

born, 36

clouds, 92

dark, 22

day, 103

dinosaurs, 141

Earth, 68

eggs, 34

food, 8

force, 116

fossil, 146

gases, 82

gravity, 129

grow, 4

hatch, 34

healthy, 6

heat, 102

insects, 58

land, 65

lifts, 129

light, 22

liquids, 80

living, 68

magnets, 133

mammals, 36

mammoth, 142

matter, 76

move, 31

night, 103

parents, 32

plants, 16

pull, 114

push, 114

rains, 90

saber-toothed
cat, 144

seeds, 18

soil, 26

solids, 78

Sun, 95

tar pools, 149

water, 21

wheels, 121

young, 38

A 3
B 4
C 5
D 6
E 7
F 8
G 9
H 0
I 1
J 2